Memories
and
Meditations

Memories
and
Meditations

By
Leon Fallis Kenney

Decorations
by Peggie Bach

THE WESTMINSTER PRESS
Philadelphia

Book Design by Dorothy Alden Smith

Published by The Westminster Press ®
Philadelphia, Pennsylvania

PRINTED IN THE UNITED STATES OF AMERICA

Library of Congress Cataloging in Publication Data

Kenney, Leon Fallis.
    Memories and meditations.

    1. Aged—Prayer-books and devotions—English.
I. Title.
BV4580.K46   248'.85   76–46643
ISBN 0–664–21290–5

This little book is lovingly dedicated to Ruth, whom I have loved and whose love has meant so much to me for about three quarters of our lives

CONTENTS

HOW TO ENJOY THIS BOOK

First of all, enjoy my blessings for having made the purchase which makes you a patron of the arts.

I have used the following pages as an expression of my love for my wife, our children, our grandchildren and great-grandchildren. Maybe it will facilitate your expression of feelings—so try reading it to your spouse. Maybe it will have some meaning for your "special days." Keep your copy to reread in another sitting and buy a copy for one of your good friends.

If you don't like what you read here, give the book to someone you dislike. Or, even better, recommend the book to that person. You will have a kind of sadistic satisfaction, and the publisher will be happy for a wider distribution of his product.

Anyone who receives a copy as a gift will not quite know your motive for giving it. In this way you stimulate guessing and add a little spice to life. Who knows, you may be the inspiration which helps him or her to try to shape up and become a person anyone can like.

We do hope that we have outlined some eternal truths, have given you a little fun, and most of all supplied a lift that comes from a positive attitude toward life and family.

Mixed Blessings

So we come to retirement—what's it all about?

Retirement is much more than a gold watch and a pension.

Retirement is a time of transition, when we leave one way of life and enter upon a new way of living.

Retirement is an adjustment involving many facets of life: financial, physical, social, recreational, and possibly theological.

Retirement is a time for reevaluation of our attainments, aspirations, and priorities.

Retirement is how we deal with having unlimited time for varied activities but limited finance or strength for participation in them.

Retirement is going back to the old place of employment and having a warm glow as you are greeted with affection, but also having a cold feeling which comes from knowing you are no longer a part of it all.

Retirement is a time of losing some old friends and members of the family but growing closer to remaining friends and family.

Retirement is finding that when a door is closed on the past, another opens on the future.

Retirement is gratitude for the old and hope for the new.

For Better, For Worse . . .

The wife of a retired man said: "According to the marriage service, I took my husband for better, for worse, for richer, for poorer. But I don't recall anything about having him home for lunch every day!" Some wives do find that having their men home all day, every day, is just too much.

Some of these husbands offer suggestions and help in areas in which they have no expertise: cooking, housework, and even fancywork. These poor fellows who miss their former daily schedule keep getting in the way of the busy homemaker who knows her job. Some of them interrupt well-established routines because they want to play a game of pinochle or gin

rummy. They don't want the vacuum cleaner running during ball games.

Some wives make the adjustment. They retire along with their men. They relinquish some of the chores. The two of them work together, cleaning, cooking, doing dishes in *their* house. Respecting each other, they learn to love each other even more deeply and find retirement a second honeymoon. Sharing house and yard chores, they have more time to do things together. They can pursue old and new hobbies and crafts. As volunteers they can meet the needs of others as well as their own.

One wife told me that she enjoys going out to dinner with her husband, just the two of them having a leisurely meal. She finds it more relaxing than going to the club, to a church, or to a social gathering. "There's a warm security in knowing his love." A husband whom we see frequently at the steakhouse said of his wife: "She got up every morning for forty-five years to get my breakfast. Now she can retire too."

A Vermont farmer once said, "I love my wife so much I can hardly keep from telling her." Why keep the secret? *Tell* her.

God's Watching!

A number of years ago we lived in a beautiful town in Massachusetts. Its beauty lay not only in that which nature had to offer but in its lovely and lovable people. The church had a lively group of high-school-age youngsters. They were spirited kids who had a lot of fun in life. One of their stunts was to drive along the town's "Lovers' Lane," pull up beside a parked car, and startle an amorous couple with a unison chant: "God's watching!"

It was an early 1930's version of Maude's statement, "God will get you for that!"

This idea of God used to scare the daylights out of me when I was a youngster. It is pretty terrible to think

of God as a divine "Peeping Tom in the Skies," who spent his time keeping a score sheet on which he tallied up the punishments I had coming.

This morning I watched a pair of sparrows who were busy building a nest. They gathered twigs, dried grass, and pieces of string which I had draped over the fence. They looked as if they felt secure and "bird happy" as they awaited a new family.

Somehow, seeing them, I felt I was more secure and "person happy." The words of an old hymn flashed to mind: "His eye is on the sparrow, and I know he's watching me." He's not keeping score, he's taking care.

Holidays

I have finally figured out why I haven't liked holidays since I retired. All my neighbors can stay home from their jobs, but I don't have any job to stay home from.

During my working years I clutched holidays to my bosom like the father who welcomed home the prodigal son. Holidays had great meaning: a family trip to the beach, a visit with friends or relatives, the family staying home and sharing in some meaningful project. Sometimes a holiday meant sleeping late, going without a shave, and not having to wear a tie. Holidays were a change of pace.

Holidays can be a change even in retirement. They may be a time to dress up: to wear shoes in place of sneakers, to put on double knits rather than chinos, to

wear a shirt and tie rather than a sweatshirt. They may even mean having a shave at the crack of dawn and adding a little "I needed that."

I read of some Jews who volunteered to take a longer work shift so that their Christian friends could enjoy a family observance of Christmas. In the same way we could make an added effort on holidays so that other families could have a better day. We could man the information desk at the local hospital, or work in the gift shop, or push wheelchairs; or babysit so some mother would be free to play tennis with her husband.

Using your imagination, your skills, and your opportunities, you could expand this into a long list. You have your own special contribution to make.

We may then all sing, "Holidays can be happy days!"

A Dismal Day

Today is one of those days, a combination of foggy drizzle and cold almost to the freezing point. This is the kind of day when retirement seems like a very good idea. No job demands our leaving the house. We can stay in and get a few of the house chores done. And I'll probably get a case of cabin fever and grumble about what the weatherman has dished up.

This morning's newspaper was wrapped in a plastic bag when it was thrown into the yard, but it landed in just the right position to soak up the water running down toward the street. A soggy newspaper, ugh!

Trying to make just one trip to the mailbox, I waited too long and missed the mailman, who had driven

off before I could give him some letters I wanted to mail.

This dampness makes my arthritis worse and stiffens me. Why did we ever move to this area and its wet climate?

Wait a bit! Didn't I used to sing, "It isn't raining rain, you know, it's raining violets"? Without the cold my apple tree won't bear. Without the rain my lawn would dry up and blow away.

Bill Stidger, a former pastor in Boston, wrote a poem, "I saw God wash the world last night and hang it out to dry." Noah finally saw the rainbow, and I guess we are in for a much shorter spell of rain than that old patriarch endured.

Having an Affair?

Ann Landers has a tremendous following. If you are one of her readers, you have probably seen the letter submitted by a woman who tells why she is having a wonderful time with "another man":

He always smells good.

He acts as if he is interested in what I have to say.

Whenever he sees me, his first words are something like, "You look wonderful," or "I've been counting the minutes."

He has a warm sense of humor and makes me laugh.

He never yells at me, even when I deserve it.

He takes my arm when we cross the street.

He never seems to notice other women when he's with me.

23

He often telephones just to say, "I'm thinking about you, dear."

He always checks the car door and locks it so I won't fall out.

He never lies to me even though he could probably get away with it.

He lets me know I am an important part of his life.

I wonder why she had to find this gallant lovemaking outside her marriage. There is nothing suggested in her list that a thoughtful husband wouldn't have offered. Why is it that we tend to take so much for granted? Why do we assume that, because we have taken a mate at the altar, we no longer need to give voice to our feelings of love?

In a joking way my father used to sum it up, "You don't run for a streetcar after you have caught it." But family love is no streetcar—it's a vehicle that needs to be refueled frequently. Acts and words of love are not affected by inflation; they cost so little when they come from the heart. Have an affair with your spouse!

Banking for the Winter

My paternal grandparents started their life together in a small wooden house in Rhode Island. It only cost $700 for six rooms (three up and three down). There was a well-beaten path to the "necessity house" out back. (One wonders if those Chick Sales buildings with the customary Sears catalog are where someone got the idea of a catalog store.)

As they prospered, my grandparents added a lean-to kitchen built on several brick pillars. To keep animals from getting under the kitchen, they installed a latticework frame around the base of the room. This was great for summer cooling, but it left much to be desired in a New England winter, when the waterpipes to and

from the sink were vulnerable to the freezing blasts.

Grandpa worked it out. He weatherstripped the kitchen crawlway by banking the lattice with piles of leaves held in place by pine boughs. In spite of his precautions there were times when the cold got the better of the waterpipes. Not to be daunted, Grandpa —in his seventies and eighties—met the challenge head on. He would pull the banking aside and crawl in under the frozen pipes, and thaw them out with a kettle of boiling water. Believe it or not, that old house is still standing. I think it is rather proud that it served the family for a century and a third.

If I were moralizing (which of course I am), I could draw a lesson from that story. First: We can bank against coming difficulties and prepare to meet them. Our banks can be finances, family, great friendships, and spiritual resources. Second: We older folks can be like Grandpa—when he couldn't walk in to do the job, he could at least crawl and make use of what he had at hand. We may join foresight with now-action.

A Blotter?

One of the delights of being old is being visited by the young.

Recently one of the small fry in our family was at our home in Liberty, Missouri. Trying to let this twelve-year-old see all the sights, I took him to the Bank Museum.

This bank was the scene of the first daylight bank robbery in the United States. Frank and Jesse James are believed to have been the leaders of the holdup men.

The hostess is a most gracious lady and she seemed anxious that the lad should see all the interesting items. He appeared quite puzzled when she showed him a shaker used to sprinkle sand on freshly written pages. He didn't understand, nor did it clear things up for him when she explained that this was an early form of blotter.

Raymond has grown up in the age of the ballpoint and the felt-tip pen, neither of which requires a blotter.

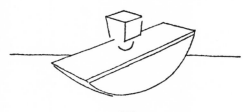

His reaction makes us realize that all too many of the things which may mean a lot to us oldsters have no significance to newer generations. People, places, and events that are dear to *us* may be completely outside *their* interest and experience. It may even be that some of our opinions and even our convictions may well be ours alone, and should not be foisted upon others. Each generation must find its own set of values and beliefs. We should not be surprised if they differ from our own. They may even be better.

. . . Replenish the Earth . . .

A front-page story in the *St. Paul Dispatch* (October 16, 1975) showed a beautiful orchid, the *Calypso Bulbosa,* one of twelve species found growing in a forty-acre bog in the Chippewa National Forest. Conservationists are keeping the location a close secret for fear that thoughtless and careless tourists would soon ruin the natural habitat if they were allowed in. It says something about the American public.

Perhaps you and I get all uptight thinking of people who would ruin an orchid bog, who would despoil one of nature's treasure troves. We can be pretty judgmen-

tal unless we take time to ask ourselves how much we have contributed to the tons of trash tossed out of car windows, scattered at picnic spots, or dropped by the stream where we were fishing.

The story of Creation in Genesis says that God was pleased with his handiwork, calling it "good." He was pleased with people, and entrusted his world to their keeping with a charge to take good care of his world. We "had it made." Such a bountiful heritage we were given! But we have a tendency to be grabbers rather than good stewards.

The orchid bog story is a plea to us to value highly what we have been given and take care of it.

Tumbledown Barns

There is something sad about buildings being allowed to fall apart, victims of time and neglect. How proud the farmer was when his neighbors joined him in a barn raising—providing shelter for his livestock and a storage place for his harvests! A good trig barn proclaimed the farmer to be an industrious man who was proud of his place in the sun.

Drive along the highway today and you may see many a barn which is merely a pile of rotting boards and timbers. You will also see the shells of old farmhouses which have met the same fate as the barns. These battered houses used to be homes in which families knew love and happiness. Children played in the yards and wives cared tenderly for flowers and vegeta-

31

ble gardens. These homes, if used at all, now only store a few tons of hay.

What stories these old wrecks could tell! They were needed; they were a source of family pride. But times have changed. Grain now goes to the elevator and it isn't profitable to keep livestock. The families need larger homes with "modern conveniences"—so why keep up the old relics?

It reminds me of the story about the oldster who was in the waiting room shared by patients of the M.D. and the D.D.S. The dentist appeared and motioned for him to come on in. But the old man declined, saying, "Not until I see the M.D., to see if it's worth having all that dental work done."

If we put off those needed trips to the doctor, or the barber, or even the clothing store, we are placing ourselves in the category of the old barn. Self-neglect accelerates the rate of decay.

The Words of My Mouth . . .

The author of Psalm 19 ended that gem with a prayer that his words might always be acceptable. We may share the psalmist's sentiment, but those of us who grew up in another generation have a particular problem: words don't mean the same thing anymore.

We could get into trouble if we describe a dear friend as "gay." "Fuzz" is no longer that hairy covering on a peach. On returning from a vacation you don't tell your friends that you have had "a good trip." You have to be careful how you use the word "pot"—you might be investigated by a narcotics agent. A "pusher" is no longer an industrious man who puts his back to the wheel. Going "main line" no longer means that you

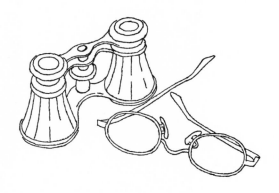

avoid a branch line on a railroad.

A "heist" is not what you need when you feel your trousers slipping. A "doll" is not a toy with which a little girl plays. The "slammer" isn't the lad who is careless about the way he shuts the door. "Busted" means neither that a man has lost his money, nor that a woman is frontally well endowed. To "drag" is quite the opposite of the way a little boy moves his feet as he heads toward school. The "establishment" is no longer seen as the preserver of society, but as the strangler. A "flower girl" isn't a sweet little tot who precedes the bride in the wedding processional; she's a dropout from society.

No wonder our grandchildren look askance when we use the old words to make a reasonable pitch (new word for "suggestion"). Early Christians were admonished to be as wise as serpents and as harmless as doves. That's what we have to be as we try to walk and talk in two worlds.

Let Go!

Barnaby Jones, the affable television private detective, gave the following advice to an acquaintance: "Troubles are like babies: the more you nurse them, the larger they grow."

Some parents are not content with having breast-fed a child. They "hang on" to their children and figuratively nurse them throughout their lives. These children are told every move to make, and when and how and where. They grow up physically, but may turn into emotional dwarfs who are afraid to make any decisions on their own. Such parents, of course, would be the first to deny possessiveness; they will explain that they want to "do all they can" for their children.

We should pay attention to our children and give

them the love and protection they need. But there comes that time when, for their sakes and for ours, we have to let them be themselves. We have to let go in spite of the "empty nest" and all that means to parents.

There are also times when people clutch their troubles to their breasts with equal passion. Their "beloved symptom" seems to be needed. Troubles are conversation pieces, reasons for complaining, and tools for getting attention or sympathy. Sometimes they serve as excuses for our failures in life and love—or our laziness.

Troubles, like babies, need attention. We have to do something about them. But then we have to let them go—and start building our lives on the positive side of the ledger.

Together in *Simches*

Ann Landers quotes an old Yiddish promise made to friends and relatives: "We will get together in *simches.*" *Simches* means "happy occasions."

This was written in response to a letter telling of the overwhelming grief of a man who "never had the time or the money" to visit his brother. When his brother died, he dug up the money to go to the funeral. He was plagued with guilt over his years of neglect.

We older folks enjoy having family and friends drop in for a visit. It's strange how much better a cup of coffee tastes when it is shared. We can't put all the burden of responsibility on others. We must make people feel welcome and we must do our share of visiting.

One of the curses of retirement is isolation. We have left the place of employment and all the associates there. Even if we go back, things are not the same, for we are no longer involved in the function of our old place of business. The old associates greet us as friends, but we are no longer colleagues. We really can't go back—we must live in the here and the now.

It is important that we stand by our neighbors, friends, and family when they are passing through difficult times. I believe that we can best accomplish this helping relationship if we have laid a foundation of fellowship in happy times. How can we share our hurts if we have never learned to share our acceptance of, confidence in, and mutual respect for one another?

In short: "We will get together in *simches.*"

Criteria of Emotional Maturity

"Oh, come on, grow up!" has been said to many a person, suggesting that the speaker thinks the other is childish.

Land only knows how many senior citizens have grown up physically. We have gone through all the stages of growth, and now some of us are beginning to "grow down," getting a little shorter in stature and stamina. But "growing up" is not the only maturity. Have we grown to an *emotional* maturity?

The Menninger Foundation once printed an appealing card detailing the "Criteria of Emotional Maturity." It is worthy of wide distribution. Emotional maturity means:

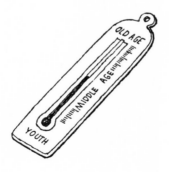

Having the ability to deal constructively with reality.

Having the capacity to adapt to change.

Having a relative freedom from symptoms produced by tensions and anxieties.

Having the capacity to find more satisfaction in giving than in receiving.

Having the capacity to relate to other people in a consistent manner with mutual satisfaction and helpfulness.

Having the capacity to sublimate, to direct one's instinctive hostile energy into creative and constructive outlets.

Having the capacity to love.

This is a challenge to us. We should keep this emotional thermometer handy so we can check ourselves. Even in old age we can still grow in mind, spirit, and interpersonal relationships.

. . . Your Longevity?

"To what do you attribute your longevity?" This seems to be the stock question which reporters ask when their editors have told them to write up a human interest story on some oldster. Special diets, avoiding alcohol or tobacco, plenty of exercise, or keeping emotionally calm—these are but a few of the many answers.

While in Tombstone, Arizona, we asked that wiry oldster, Idaho Ellison, how he maintained his youthful appearance. He said, "I never drank, never smoked, and never went out with wild women until I was twelve years of age."

A recent cartoon by Hoest shows an old man being interviewed by the local correspondent. The caption reads, "I attribute my long life to canceling my ocean voyage on the *Lusitania* back in 1915."

My grandfather carried a gold-handled cane which was entrusted to him by a Boston newspaper. It designated him as the oldest living man in his town. The family used to say that eventually we would have to shoot Gramps to get him ready for Resurrection Day.

I suppose there are many, many things which contribute to longevity; but there is so much more to our goal than to live long. Be it long or short, the quality of life is measured by what we have done and are doing with the years granted us. It is not what we have received but what we are contributing. It is not what we enjoy but how much joy we bring to others.

The Clydesdales

For a couple of years, we lived in an apartment that looked out onto the field where August Busch pastured his famed Clydesdale horses. For years we had seen the television commercial in which those majestic animals pulled the brewery wagon through the impressive gates at Grant's Farm. We had to adjust our thinking when we saw these animals as frisky colts galloping across a field. It was hard to think of them as coming up to the fence to have their noses rubbed, or to see them taking a handful of tender grass from admiring children.

I wonder if we don't type people in much the same way—finding it hard to change our first impressions. We are prone to see folks in a stylized role. Sometimes

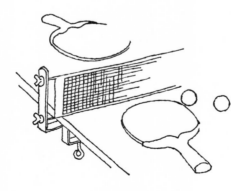

the role we cast them in is the one which we feel is proper for their station or their occupation.

I found it refreshing to see President Truman at the piano. It is good to see the local doctor and his family on a float trip or out on skis. The pastor looks more human in sweaty shorts as he cuts his grass. It is encouraging to see the local banker playing ping-pong with as much concentrated effort as one would expect in an Olympics contest.

Stereotypes are limiting and dehumanizing. There is more to all persons than the roles we assign them. We should feel free to do our own thing, and let others do theirs.

Vacation

During the war there was a mixup in requisition orders, and the ship's crew were served turkey every day for over a month. A friend of ours said that after that experience it took him years to enjoy a Thanksgiving turkey dinner.

While I was in college I waited on tables in a restaurant which served the help T-bone steaks one night and pork tenderloins the next. It was great eating, but I looked forward to getting home to one of my mother's corned beef dinners. A steady diet of turkey, T-bones, or tenderloins? No way!

Retirement might be called a steady diet of vacation.

A steady, repetitious sequence of events, even the most pleasant events, can get you down. A recent issue of *Retirement Advisor* carried two pages of vacation "how-tos":

"Now that spring is approaching, many folks begin to think about making vacation plans. We've found, however, that a large number of retired people feel that since they are no longer working, they no longer need a vacation. Medical experts point out that nothing can be farther from the truth. Vacations can contribute to good health as well as raise the spirits."

One of the patients at the state hospital where I worked was discharged to live in a nursing home. At the end of her first year "on the outside" she told her social worker that she wanted a vacation. She packed her bag and came back to the hospital for a couple of weeks with her old friends. After her vacation she returned to the nursing home and found contentment.

Haven't you said, "Oh, how good it is to be home!" on returning from a vacation? Get out of the rut for a while and it will be more comfortable after a vacation.

Death Notices

Some articles on "Death with Dignity" got me interested enough to comb local papers for a month to see how people die. I didn't come up with statistics based upon exhaustive research, but rather with a set of impressions. Nearly all the middle-aged and older group died in a hospital or a nursing home. I gave up counting, as there was rarely a diagnosis—except that the following kept appearing in the accounts: heart, cancer, long illness, and a rash of 26 encephalitis deaths. It was rare indeed to see one listed as having died at home.

Industry would appear to have protected its workers, for there were but five industrial deaths listed. On the other hand, it would appear that danger lurks around those at play: 19 drowned; 5 died in a cave-in; one each died by suffocation in an icebox, by being killed by a

bear, a crocodile, a swarm of bees, lightning, a pitched ball; and one was hit by a golf club.

Transportation appears dangerous: 46 died in one-car accidents and 39 in two-car accidents; 14 died on motorbikes, and one each on bicycle and motor scooter. Pedestrians were endangered, as 13 (including a roadside construction flagman) were killed while on foot. Three died in stock car races. Three fell from a car or truck. Four hundred died in China in a boat collision, and several air crashes accounted for 254 deaths.

Man also lifted his hand against his fellowman: 24 were shot, 11 stabbed, 8 killed by guerrilla action, 6 in bombings, and one each by sword wound, beating, strangulation, fist fight, ax murder, and a booby trap. There were 9 suicides.

Conclusion: It seems to be safe at work, safer at home, and safest at church. So, let's get with it.

The Older Generation

My mother loved to entertain, and her home was a mecca for all my maternal cousins, aunts, and uncles. She always served the Thanksgiving and Christmas dinner! On the Fourth of July, the whole family gathered on her front porch to watch the gala parade. On these festive days my father's relatives visited or came to see the parade. My father died while I was in college, but Mother kept up the traditional festive board and open house.

Each year the assembly dwindled as one or another

of the older generation died. Mother kept on and on. It was just before one Thanksgiving that she died. Our immediate family sat down to a rather spiritless Thanksgiving dinner, still in the shock of our grief.

We had many blessed memories to share. Past joys and former festive days seemed to haunt us like Scrooge's "Ghost of Christmas Past." Part of normal grief is a feeling of guilt. We regretted that we had not done more to make mother's life easier. But there was an additional dimension to our grief, and it came like a bolt out of the blue. It was the sudden realization that "We are now the older generation." Could we accept this fact?

It was a sobering experience which presented a challenge. Would we, the new members of the older generation, have the desire and the ability to build pleasant memories for our children and our children's children? We decided that a "good memory bank" was the best heritage which we could leave them. How we succeed we will probably never know, but we live and die trying.

Wearing Another's Moccasins

There's an old Indian saying that we can never understand another man until we have worn his moccasins. It is so terribly easy to be critical, or to lack understanding of another person when we don't know all the factors of his situation. Allow me to use the following personal illustration.

When I was a relatively young man there were two older men with whom I was closely associated. One was my beloved father-in-law and the other was the senior pastor (and later pastor emeritus) of the church that I served. I owed much to these two men: one had given

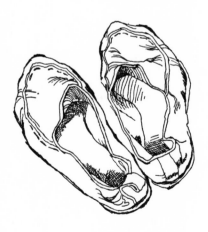

me his daughter, and the other had given me a solid foundation for my life's work. As the years slipped by, these men seemed to become careless in their appearance. You could often see little tufts of gray whiskers which they had missed while shaving.

Their apparent carelessness bothered me more than it should have. It was probably due to my unwillingness to see any flaw in either of the men who had meant so much in my life. In home and in church they had helped shape my way of living, both personal and professional.

Now my hair is gray and so is my beard. I understand them far better than I did before. Though I am very careful and double-shave with one of those new razors which never say "Gotcha," I frequently find that I have left little tufts of gray hair. I don't have their moccasins but I do have their beards.

No Place to Go

His relatives are frequent targets for the wit of comedian Rodney Dangerfield. In one monologue he told of attending the funeral of his uncle: "There he was, the atheist, all dressed up and no place to go."

This strikes at the heart of a religious belief of many cultures. Through the ages we have been unable to think of death as the end of our existence. "Holy writings" have held the promise that there is more than our apparently allotted years. Many and varied are the arguments favoring a continued existence.

There are also varying concepts of "life after death."

Some see immortality through earthbound eyes, so that it seems reasonable that continued existence would be through reincarnation, even if the returning person should be given a different physical form. Others can believe in another world of existence but one which is dependent upon the personal needs we now have. These needs are met by sending the deceased into the new life accompanied by slaves, family members, food, and symbols of wealth. Some look for a bodily resurrection of the dead. Others think of the departed as living spirits in the "other world." Some feel that immortality is best achieved in the contributions we make to future generations, our emotional, intellectual, and spiritual heirs.

Dangerfield's uncle with no place to go makes us uncomfortable. A belief in a good and loving God gives us incentive to prepare for an opportunity for a continuation of life and growth in his presence. We may not know the answers but we have a confidence.

The Ifands

We had not been acquainted with the ifands until we heard a friend say, "The sale of our house is dependent upon a lot of ifands—if we find a buyer who likes this neighborhood, and if he can get a loan, and if we can buy a better house, and if its price is lower than our selling price."

That sale is comparable to a life which makes all its progress in moves based upon conditional commitments. Such a life drags itself out in a series of ironclad guarantees rather than being a great venture of faith. Petty fears and ifands become a straitjacket making it impossible to embrace beautiful potentials.

Christopher Columbus didn't check to see if Lloyds of London was underwriting his trip—he set sail knowing the risks. The Pilgrims were never promised a bed of roses—they had a faith that they wanted to proclaim. The signers of the Declaration of Independence shared Patrick Henry's commitment to "liberty or death." Susan B. Anthony had no shield to ward off the ridicule which would be heaped upon her, but she never spared herself as she sought the right of suffrage for women. George Washington Carver didn't wait for a Federal grant for his education; he earned an Iowa State degree which provided the skills for his benevolent life.

A vibrant religion has its foundation in that kind of total commitment to a belief. It is betting your life on a faith which cannot be proved in a test tube, but only in a sense of being in tune with the Eternal Truth.

Go Home and Learn Something

Chest pains, visits to the doctor's office, routine tests in the local hospital, and more sophisticated testing in another hospital added up to a poor health report. The consensus was that I was a poor risk even for the surgery which seemed indicated. I was lucky to be well enough to endure the examinations.

The family doctor set up a protective hedge around my life. I was ordered to give up an interim pastorate in a church I dearly loved. I was to stay in the house on cold days. I could only come downstairs once a day. My new diet was a radical change; what used to be a good-night snack became a whole day's ration. Medi-

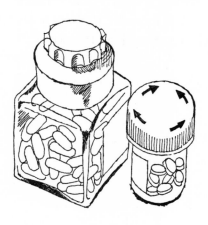

cine became a new way of life. As a machine runs on bearings I was to run on pills.

I was in a blue funk. Depression took a strong grip on me. I had always taught that a person can continue to enjoy the experience of growth, learning even in the last struggles of death. But suddenly the chips were down. I could see no good in what had befallen me. There was no light at the end of the tunnel.

My perceptive doctor sensed my depression, and seemed to sense my philosophy when he suggested that I "go home and learn something."

What I learned was difficult. Some things we can't manage but have to accept. The options still open to me had diminished, but they had not disappeared. There were still possibilities for learning and growth.

At this writing, a year and a half have passed. I'm driving my car, attending meetings, doing some preaching, traveling a little. Plato suggests that studies cleanse the soul. I have learned anew that all life is a gift for which we should be thankful.

Celebrating the New Year

Somehow, I can't get excited about wearing a funny hat and blowing a tin horn at the stroke of midnight on the thirty-first of December. There comes a time when the doctor rules out tempting desserts, hearty foods, and the champagne which tradition associates with the celebration of the New Year. We are grateful that we now live in the Midwest, where it is only eleven o'clock when Guy Lombardo ushers in the New Year back in New York. I can kiss my wife and wish her a "Happy New Year," and still get a decent night's rest.

They tell us that we have seen more new things in our generation than there were innovations in the thousand years prior to our birth. Ours has been a marvelous age in which to live. In spite of our tendency to hark

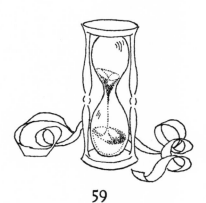

back to "the good old days" each new year shows us better and better ways to live.

New technological skills have brought us vast improvements in medical care, modes of living, working conditions, comfort in travel, and ease in communications. With all the change, it is interesting to note that they haven't come up with any new "sins." Most of the vices were well established long before we were born. The changes have occurred in the fields of education, individual rights, and creature comforts. Believing this, we can join in singing Philip Doddridge's "hymn for the new year," and share in his positive proclamation:

"Thy goodness all our hopes shall raise,
Adored, through all our changing days."

It *Is* More Blessed to Give

Inflation and the fixed income of a pension combine to make us tighten our financial belts. Even though there are causes that we would like to support (the church, our schools, service organizations), our means are limited.

A medium-sized garden is a remarkable resource. Properly cared for, a garden will do wonderful things. My last garden enabled us to express our love and appreciation to many friends and our family. Vegetables from our little plot of ground went on the tables of twenty-nine different families. It was a good feeling to be able to have them enjoy our "just-picked vegetables."

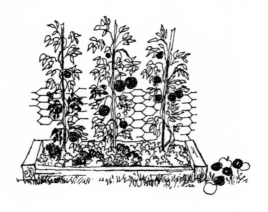

There is no need for inflation to deflate our generosity. There is no price tag on some of the most meaningful gifts which we can give. Youngsters need the gift of love and companionship, such as that offered through the Big Brother program. Scout troops can use the newspapers we save. In our neighborhood, a boys club is happy to have our grass clippings, which they sell for mulch. Young people need our interest and encouragement in their programs of sports, dramatics, and music. A few hours of baby-sitting is appreciated by young married couples. The old and the sick appreciate a few flowers, and short visits which break the sameness of the sickroom. Using your imagination, you can dream up a raft of "good gifts" to be made in addition to the time spent in the usual volunteer programs.

The strange part of it all is that when we give something to someone else we have given ourselves the best gift of all—the satisfaction of having done a good thing.

God Loves You

When I retired, my fellow workers gave a nice party and some wonderful farewell gifts. One card read, "Even dirty old men need love." At first that card was just a "funny" about which we all could laugh. Later, it became clear that it showed remarkable insight. Retirement is the closing of a person's major, and lifelong, contribution to society. The pay which a person has earned is of secondary importance to knowing that the way a job was done was worthy of the pay which was received. The fact that someone is willing to pay for your work is evidence that you are a needed and worthwhile person. The need for such assurance continues after the paycheck stops.

Too many people are inhibited about expressing their

feelings. It is very hard for some folks to tell someone that they really care. Some churches have an active ritual of fellowship. It is good for members of the congregation to take time to shake the hand of someone nearby and to say, "God loves you, and so do I."

This implies a love different from that expressed by a paycheck "for services rendered." It helps to point us to an awareness that we are loved for what we are, or ("miracle of miracles") that we are loved for what we can become.

A paycheck is gone in a very few days, but Paul says that of the abiding values, love is the greatest. Who are some of the people you appreciate and care about? Have you told them lately?

What's Cooking?

A local paper announced that the university extension service had prepared a booklet on "Cooking for Two." The service was flooded with eleven thousand requests for copies. That many responses from a single announcement indicates that there is a widespread need for help.

When the flu confined my wife to bed the problem of cooking became more obvious to me. It has been a long time since all our dining chairs were filled with regularity. We can't buy the way we used to. A big roast, or a turkey, might fit our oven, but it would give

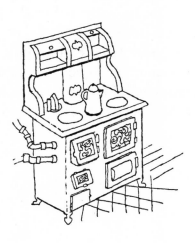

us fits trying to eat the whole thing. It would appear that the supermarket thinks every family is made up of a dozen lumberjacks. Even if we wanted the "giant super package," how often would a pension permit such purchases?

As the years roll on, they tend to leave their wheel-marks on our aging bodies. Having danced through mounds of culinary delights, we must now pay the piper. These special diets don't encourage us to be gourmet chefs. (Would that I had lived before they invented calories and cholesterol.) What work it is to balance a diet with a blend of nourishment, appetizing appearance, and a proper respect for the budget! Thank God for what Meals On Wheels is offering, especially when the person who makes the delivery has time to "sit a spell."

When I'm alone I tend to cut corners on the cooking chores. One-pan meals, eaten out of the pan, tend to be the norm. I am not enamored of doing dishes, but so far I have not been tempted to cook a chop in the toaster to save washing the frying pan. I guess that this cooking business is one of the ways which we can check on ourselves to see that we don't let down but keep up our standards.

The Family Story

Older people have a rich, nostalgic memory bank. Members of the younger generation don't know what they are missing if they don't want to hear those choice little tidbits which their elders have to share.

Someone has written that the old family stories are not fully appreciated until you are fifty—and by then those who wanted to tell the stories have gone. With this in mind I wrote a family storybook telling about my hometown and the members of the family and how they lived. I added a section about the places where I have worked, and another about people I have known and events I remembered. Publication was limited to four Xeroxed copies—one for my wife and one for each of my three children.

It was gratifying to have my son say that he stayed up all night to read it, and for my daughter to say that she and her family were "all choked up with a feeling of fondness." I believe there is a real value in preserving such things for our children and our children's children. Some of us find it easier to express our feelings in writing.

It is said that ours is an impersonal age. Many people suffer identity problems. Families scatter and relationships become casual. Perhaps some means of communicating our innermost feelings to those who count so much in our lives could supply a missing ingredient. The family story might make a contribution to stability and health.

A Hobby

Just about everyone who has written about retirement has suggested that having a hobby helps makes life more enjoyable. It is next to impossible to suggest a good hobby for another person. The main criterion for a hobby is personal enjoyment.

A collection may be made of anything which interests you and which you can afford. Some collections cost little more than time and imagination, while others (such as antique cars) are terribly expensive. I remember asking a lady if her husband had bought any new stamps for his collection. She bristled as she said,

"I've been needing a set of false teeth for twenty-five years—but he's been buying stamps!"

Learning a craft is fun. At little cost you may make gifts for your family and friends. At sixty-six I attended tole painting classes and learned a lot—especially that I'm no Rembrandt. Physical hobbies keep you fit in body and mind. A neighbor spices up his daily walks by stopping at every house to put either the morning or the evening paper on the porch. If he misses a day, the whole neighborhood is concerned about him. Making a hobby of gaining knowledge or of using it gives a lot of joy. A recent medical report stated that those who keep mentally active tend to live longer.

An extra dividend of having a hobby is joining a group with the same hobby. This means widening your circle of friends at a time when, for many older people, the circle is shrinking. Old friends are good but one new friend can be marvelous as well. Why not read the opportunity column instead of the obituaries?

Sensing the Eternal

We have friends in Arizona who taught us how to get the most enjoyment out of viewing a brilliant sunset. When conditions are right for a particularly good sky show, they drive out to the edge of town to the crest of a hill where they may enjoy an unobstructed panorama of color. Between them and the skies there are no factories, no telephone poles, no television antennas, not even a single house. Nothing that man has made stands between them and the handiwork of the divine artist. At best, the view lasts but a few minutes; but it has a way of etching

a glorious memory that brightens the coming night and the days to follow.

Now and again we learn of those rare saints who dwell in the Presence—but most of us are given only fleeting glimpses of the Eternal. Life gets so cluttered with the important and the unimportant that we fail to provide a quiet time for contemplation. Every day brings necessary involvements with family, friends, neighbors, and acquaintances. The very business of living claims our concentration. Problems, personal and interpersonal, make incessant demands on our time. All sorts of immediate preoccupations crowd our horizons —blotting out the vision.

How good it is, even in the midst of toil and confusion, to find a few moments when we can be alone in the stillness with our God. Make time for sensing the marvels of the Eternal.

One Nation Under God

In classrooms all across the country, schoolchildren repeat the Pledge of Allegiance, which includes the phrase "One nation under God." Numerous patriotic gatherings are opened with the same statement. This can be meaningless cant, a semipious nod in the direction of a boring tradition; or it can be a recognition of the part which the Lord has played in our country's history. It is whatever happens in the mind of the person making the pledge.

God has been given an important place in our heritage. We even use the coin of the land to proclaim our

trust in him. Many of the colonists came to this land because they felt that here they could worship according to their convictions. These were hardworking and hardheaded men and women who took their faith seriously. Having built their homes and their meetinghouses, they next built a college, that their clergymen might have sound minds as well as sound faith.

This country has been described as a "melting pot," but religiously we might better be described as a "stew pot." Each faith group has maintained its individuality, while blending with the others in the creation of a delectable dish.

God-fearing citizens have far more of an obligation than making the Pledge of Allegiance. We become the voice of God when we commend righteous leadership, and when we protest that which is shoddy and evil.

Retirement gives us more time to read about the issues of the day, more time to write expressing our views so that legislators may have their fingers on our pulse. We can campaign on behalf of policy rather than party, for personal integrity rather than personality. Can we justify sitting at home and grumbling about public scandals if we have been scandalously absent from the polls at primary and general elections?

A Good God

A Victorian mansion with 160 rooms, in San Jose, California, is really a monument to an irrational fear. Mrs. Sarah Winchester was terrified that the spirits of Indians slain by the famed Winchester rifle would come back seeking revenge on the family of the manufacturer of the instrument of their death. To foil them in their search, she added a maze of rooms to keep them from finding their way. She even had the carpenters build stairways that led only to the ceiling.

Ashkenazic Jews in Talmudic and later times had a similar fear of evil spirits. They would never name a

child after an older living person for fear the angel of death might get mixed up: coming for an older person, the angel might take the young child of the same name (a case of having the right name but the wrong address).

Faulty theology can give rise to irrational fears and create a terrible insecurity within us. I have no place in my thinking for a God who is vengeful or capricious. The God I believe in has said, "Lo, I am with you always." He is not a God who makes mistakes, or sends evil spirits, or plucks the wrong life from amidst the living.

On the other hand, we know that *we* make mistakes. We stumble and blunder through life. But even as we stumble we remember the words of the ancient psalmist, who expressed assurance that God's angels will bear us up lest we stub our toes on a stone.

God is for us, not against us. He is dependable and unchanging, and he is good. What assurance and joy there is in trusting such a God!

A Missing Symbol

It had been a hectic day for a six-year-old. His playmates had been in for an afternoon birthday party. His maternal grandparents had arrived for the upcoming birthday. Mama had made special cupcakes, baked in ice-cream cones and frosted in different colors. These would be brought to school so his classmates could celebrate with him. His parents had given him one of the family presents. When his Dad was tucking him in for the night they discussed the events of the day. Dad said, "You don't seem really happy about it all." The little fellow sighed and said, "But . . . nobody gave me a spanking."

The next evening—the true birth anniversary—both sets of grandparents joined the celebration. We observed all the family traditions: his nose was buttered so he could slide through the new year; he was given six spanks and "one to grow on." We sang "Happy Birthday," and he blew out the candles and cut the cake himself. There were presents, and he was permitted to stay up a little later than usual—a happy boy.

The two evenings pointed up the importance of the simple amenities. It is so easy to become careless and forget that courtesy plays an important role in every relationship. Taking time (to express appreciation, to voice our concern, to say that we love) is the way to strengthen a good relationship. Where there may have been some question about the soundness of an alliance, taking time for gracious courtesy may help by demonstrating that we do care.

Taking God Home with You

There is an interesting story in the Second Book of Kings. It tells of the healing of Naaman, an important military leader from Syria. When it was discovered that he had leprosy he was directed to Elisha, the prophet of Israel. And Naaman found healing at the hands of the Lord.

In accord with an ancient superstition, Naaman thought that the God of Israel must surely dwell in the very land itself. Having found his encounter with this God to be good, he wanted to continue the relation-

ship. He asked for two mules' burden of the earth of Israel to take back to Syria, feeling that he was taking God back home with him.

In spite of widespread acceptance of the universality of God, some of us act as if the Lord was to be found only in some specific place. God may have become real and meaningful to us within a beloved church, at a summer conference, a national convention, or while making a retreat. But if he is the Lord of the universe, his meaning is not restricted to that one place or experience.

We may have a good reason for a sentimental attachment to the old church, but as nonresident members we sell short the old church as well as ourselves. It is true that we have strengthening of faith and devotion at the meetinghouse; but religion is how we live, move, and have our being. We can bring God home with us. In fact, he is always near. Wherever we are we can learn to be at home with him.

A Special Welcome

Do you remember your first day at school? It probably was a difficult experience. It involved going into a new situation, with new people and no assurance that you really belonged.

The same uncertainty, fears, and apprehension may be ours when we move into a new community, take a new job, or join a new club or group. So much depends upon the reaction of the new people with whom we come in contact.

One Saturday I served as host at the historical museum and met a fine young family who had just moved into town. I invited them to attend our church and they said they would probably be there the next day.

That evening I called the pastor and gave him the names and description of the family. They would be hard to miss: a beautiful young woman with red hair, a man with neatly trimmed black beard, and two teenagers.

As a part of the service, the pastor had started a "ritual of friendship" in which the members of the congregation greet friends and welcome strangers. This is no formal bowing or merely shaking hands; folks leave their seats to speak to one another. On this morning he said: "I see that Mr. and Mrs. . . . and their children are here today. They are new residents in the community. Please make them welcome."

Many lonely people would be less lonely if others would make the first gesture of friendship. Who is new in your community who needs the assurance that someone cares? A special welcome to a stranger expresses not only our love, but God's love as well.

Christmas Lights

It seems appropriate that decorative lighting should be a part of the annual celebration of the birth of Jesus, who called himself the light of the world. In the Gospel accounts of the Nativity, Luke says that the glory of the Lord shone round about the shepherds when they heard about his birth. Matthew said that it was a star of exceptional brilliance that led the Wise Men to the newborn Jesus.

My choice of decorations is probably influenced by the impressions I had as a youngster. My hometown was established long before the Declaration of Independence. On many a Christmas Eve it was dusted

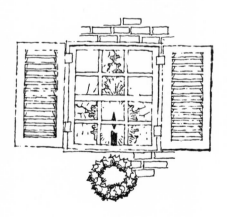

over by a covering of pristine snow which softened and beautified simple homes and mansions alike. Front window curtains were drawn aside, shades were raised, and on each windowsill a single lighted candle was placed.

Homes decorated that way were beautiful. Even more beautiful was the thought expressed. The candles symbolized hearts and homes that were open, receptive, and giving. They proclaimed that there was "room in the inn." The tapers announced that carol singers were welcome, and here they would find mulled cider, hot chocolate, and cookies.

I can almost hear the squeaking sound of carolers walking in cold snow, and a voice saying: "Let your light so shine . . ." Any decoration which can help generate the Christmas spirit is a proper use of Christmas lights.

Tricky Memories

Time, by its relentless passage, has a way of eroding some of the truth in our recollections of the past. As most mothers tend to forget the discomfort and pain of childbirth, so we have a tendency to find joy rather than sorrow as we dip into memory's well. It has been said that memories are the keepsake of the happy times which we have known.

We oldsters even find a perverse kind of enjoyment in telling about how hard it was when we were growing up during the depression. Apparently there is a kind of happiness in telling what little pay we received for doing such long hours of work. We tell about our

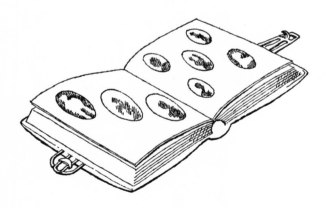

85

hardships: how poor the highways were, and what little mileage a set of tires would give. In our telling of the "hard old days" we can show off our courage, our stamina, and our winning against the odds.

We oldsters have a tendency to build up a story, embroidering the truth a bit, just to make the telling better. When we try to capture an audience by "stretching the truth," we are in danger of losing our credibility. And when we repeat the same stories over and over, we become boring.

Still, there are things that we know which deserve preservation in family tradition. The plain unvarnished truth needs no buildup. The fact is, however, that our memories play tricks on us. What we recall may not be the plain unvarnished truth, but our interpretation of it. Let us recognize that this is so and claim no more.

Great Day in the Morning

One of the most radiant men I have heard talk is a so-called terminal patient whose cancer has been arrested. He told of his way of life which includes four daily practices:

1. Each morning, rain or shine, he goes to the window and looks out on what to him is a beautiful day, as it is an added bonus which he didn't expect to have.

2. He tries, each day, to do the really important things such as expressing his love and doing acts of kindness and consideration.

3. He makes no plans for tomorrow, but spends each day in radiant living.

4. Each evening, he expresses gratitude in prayer for the day which the Lord has given him.

It is a peculiar commentary on us that we take life for granted until it is threatened. We have a tendency to procrastinate, thinking that "we will get around to . . ." those many things which we want to do or say.

A long while ago there was a suggestion made to clergymen that they should write every sermon as if it were the last they would ever be able to preach.

How much difference would it make if we were told that today is the last day we will have? How would we react? That man who had a remission of his cancer is no sob sister. He is radiant and vibrant. He is living life to the hilt and finding a great deal of happiness. That man demonstrates a way of life which need not apply only to our last few days. We can use his daily exercises even though we expect many more years.

Facing Reality

Death is not something we think much about when we are in the prime of youth. Nor does death have any charm when we possess those basic elements of life, emotional and spiritual stability, reasonable health, a good family, and a circle of friends. But death is no enemy when a person is racked by pain and faced by a mounting loss of faculties. Real death is so much kinder than a near-death which is the result of merely adding a number of days or months to existence. We all need to face up to the inevitable.

Children have a way of forcing us to be realists. We can be grateful that their ability to face the truth can

help us adults who may be living in a world of fantasy and denials.

When little Christopher came to visit he greeted me this way: "My other grandpa died, and you'll be dead soon." A few days later little Steven was visiting. He asked me to read "Little Red Riding Hood." When he turned to the picture of the grandma in bed he commented: "She's sick. She's old. She'll be dead soon. You'll be dead, Grandpa."

I helped in the church wedding for my oldest granddaughter. The second thought it would be simpler to have a home wedding with Grandpa tying the knot. The two younger sisters wondered if I could conduct a "sort of a delayed-action wedding" for them, as I will probably not be available when they are ready for their weddings.

Out of the mouths of babes often comes the truth that we may have been avoiding. The fact that life is transient makes it no less beautiful, nor does it afford us less opportunity to make a contribution to God and to our fellowman. Nor is it morbid to make provision for our own death, which is the most certain thing that lies before us.

The Will of God

When a catastrophe strikes a person or a community some well-meaning friend may try to help us by saying, "It is the will of God." This gives me no help at all. It does not strengthen my love or respect for God. To give God the blame for a shattering catastrophe is to equate God with child beaters. I have no tolerance for an adult who gives vent to his temper by beating up a child who is incapable of striking back. It is difficult to think of God venting his spleen on people who have no defense.

As I read the Gospels, I get a different picture of God and his plan for mankind. That picture comes sharply into focus in the life and ministry of Jesus, who said that he came that we might know the abundant life. He didn't claim that this was an original thought, for he was reflecting God's will and purpose. He put it

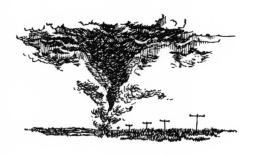

very clearly when he said, "He who has seen me has seen the Father" (John 14:9). People could see what God was like if they would pay attention to Jesus.

But catastrophes do happen. Where is God when they occur? He is not rejoicing over the affliction of people, but suffering with them, seeking to use even the most terrible experiences for good. The cross, an instrument of torture and death, became the symbol of his amazing love. It is God's will that we always experience his love and support—feeling the everlasting arms buoying us up lest we sink into despair or defeat. Jesus, who reflected God's concern, did not promise to protect us from tribulation, but that he would not forsake us when it came.

A Shattered Myth

The way in which old people are depicted by television comics, and others who think they are funny, kindles a "slow burn." Oldsters are not doddering, senseless, sexless old fools. This is not a defensive response by one who is admittedly older, it has the backing of a medical researcher.

In an address to the Medical Society of the State of New York, Stephen Nordlicht, M.D., stated that it is a misconception to believe that the elderly are bound to develop mental illness. He reported that less than one percent of those over age sixty-five are patients in mental institutions.

He suggested that with the lengthening of the life-span it is probable that by the year 2000 there will be twenty-nine million people over sixty-five. This is an increase of nine million over the number now living in

the United States. With the growing numbers, there will probably be more persons with problems of confusion and depression. But, he contends, these senior citizens are not without hope. Rather, they are candidates for the help which medicine and psychotherapy have to offer.

The doctor also expressed disapproval of the practice of removing older people from the mainstream of life. Another source suggests that 50 percent of all retirees die within two years if they are not kept busy. Dr. Nordlicht quoted Cicero's 44 B.C. statement that "old age is respected only if it asserts itself, preserves its rights, maintains its independence, and retains its way to the last breath."

Let us shatter the "doddering old fool" myth and live as fully and independently as possible.

An Advent Wreath

Having spent most of my church life in a nonliturgical denomination, it was late in my ministry before I learned to appreciate the use of an Advent wreath. I had to learn that the main component of the wreath is the cluster of five candles. On each of the Sundays of Advent (the four before Christmas) one additional candle is lighted. The fifth candle is usually at the center of the wreath and is reserved for Christmas Day. As each of the tapers is lighted, there is a brief and appropriate ritual built on the theme that we are preparing to celebrate the coming of the Light of the World.

We thought that a wreath would be fitting for the hospital chapel, but the one listed in the ecclesiastical

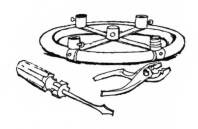

catalog was priced at $150. This was too much for the budget of the Chaplain's Division. The metal shop supervisor came to our assistance. Using odds and ends, he made a truly beautiful freestanding wreath. The wreath proper was fashioned from the handrail of a wornout wheelchair; the candle holders were made from old electric light sockets. For a few dollars and a labor of love there was a new Advent wreath in the Roman Catholic and Protestant chapels.

Many times we want something extra for a special season or family affair. When we see the price tag, and remember the balance in the checkbook, we are stopped cold. What's to stop us from using what we have? A dash of imagination, a little effort, and a bit of love is all that is needed to make something of which we are proud and others enjoy. Who needs a husky budget when you have an expansive love?

Christmastide

While driving along a St. Louis street, I saw two first-grade children climb up the slope of a front lawn. They knelt in front of the figures in the Christmas creche and said a short prayer; and having finished, they crossed themselves, and romped down the street.

I don't know the nature of their prayers, but their children's faith was beautiful to behold. Two passages of Scripture came to mind: "Let the children come to me . . ." and, "Unless you become like children . . ." Children have a way of putting it all together, without being concerned about the complexities of differing theologies.

We spent Christmas Eve at a home where theology might have been a dividing wedge, as the grandmother is a Christian and the grandfather is a Jew. It was a gala evening with good cheer and a mountain of presents.

The children were "high" during the distribution of the gifts; but the real high point of the evening was the dual family ritual. The Hanukah candles were lighted and the story was told of the saving and rededication of the Temple. Then carols were sung and the Gospel Nativity story was read.

This may sound like a mixing of conflicting traditions, but there was no conflict—love knows no divisions. Joy and goodwill abounded on every side. And why not? The God of the Jews is the God of the Christians, and he loves us all.

Peace and Quiet

As a youngster, I was upset by a section of a manual of devotions which dealt with the Final Judgment. One sentence stated that one day each person must stand alone in the awful stillness of the presence of God. I came to think of God as an all-seeing eye which knew everything that I was, and thought, and did.

The members of my family knew a lot about me, too, but they were not silent about it. Somehow I knew that even their expressions of disappointment and rebuke were meant for my own good. But this silent treatment from God sounded ominous.

In church services and youth meetings, I have noticed that people are restless during moments of silence. In therapy sessions many clients cannot tolerate quiet. Students do their homework with the hi-fi going

full blast. Many homes have a radio or television going from morning to night. We have apparently become so acclimated to noise that silence is terrifying.

Surely something significant is lost when the quiet times are crowded out of our lives. We need such times to take stock of ourselves. What is it within us that we are so reluctant to face? We need quiet times to assess the value of those things that keep us so busy and preoccupied. We need silence to hear the song of a bird, the sway of the trees in the breeze, and the happy sounds of children at play.

Often in the still, small voices we are assured that this is our Father's world, and that he is not our accuser but our strength and our hope. "Be still, and know that I am God." One way that he speaks to us is through silence. We need to be quiet often enough and long enough to get a sense of his directives for our lives.

Acquaintances or Friends?

Acquaintances are like tourists who see the points of interest but are not deeply moved by local problems. They have no share in the sweat and toil that makes for beauty, progress, and accomplishment. It is no wonder that the "natives" in the vacation spots have no great love for these visitors who are hidden behind their inevitable cameras.

Friends are like those good neighbors who share community problems and help in solving them. They are the people who get involved when trouble strikes.

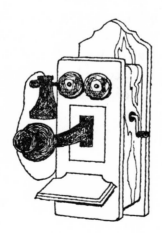

This involvement is no maudlin sentimentality; it is an honest sleeves-rolled-up-for-work concern.

One of the facts of old age is that the passing of years costs us many of our old and trusted friends. For a happier life, it behooves us to enlarge our circle of new friends. There is a sense in which new friends are a gift. There is an element of "grace" involved when other people give us their trust and their concern.

At the same time friendship is a gift that makes demands upon us. We must earn new friends in the same way we earned our dear old friends. We have to take the risk of leaving our protective shells. We have to make the effort to get acquainted with new people by using the many available opportunities to do so. We may need to create opportunities where none exist.

To have a friend, one must be a friend. Acts of neighborly kindness, gestures of thoughtfulness, expressions of interest and concern create friendship. When we share, when we trust and are trusted, then acquaintances can become loving friends. And friends are a priceless part of life.

Smile, Please!

We smile when we see the camera's lens focused on us. Some smile because it seems the natural thing to do. Others follow the photographer's suggestion when he says, "Smile, please!" The resulting pictures will suggest to posterity that we are members of a warm, friendly generation. I am quick to admit that I would rather be remembered as a nice old man than as an irascible old grouch.

The family album is just about the only place where we can get an idea of what our ancestors looked like. Two of my grandparents died before I was old enough to have known them. There is only one picture of my

paternal grandmother, and it was taken through a screen door when she happened to step to the porch. The only existing picture of my maternal grandfather is one taken in the yard in front of a bush—with the result that he looks as if there was a plume of feathers sticking out of the top of his head. My parents told me what lovely people these two were, but it was hard for me to believe it. The evidence showed a ghostlike woman and an odd-looking man with a wild headpiece.

The images that we leave for coming generations in photographs will never be as important as the impressions we have made on those who know us best. The smile on a faded photograph may disappear, but the recollection of a warm and loving person has a way of enduring. The memory portrait we leave is often formed by the little things we say and do. How we treat our friends and neighbors, the way we relate to our children and our children's children, can be part of a blessed immortality.

The Also-Rans

When I read that the Government Printing Office had issued a book *If Elected: Unsuccessful Candidates for the Presidency,* I had mixed feelings. I wondered why they should rub salt into the wounds of defeat. Then came the realization that it was not all defeat.

Thousands of men and women have aspired to public office. A small percentage won the primaries, and a smaller group won the endorsement of a political party. An even more select number were on the ballot for the Presidency. To have reached that goal was an achievement of considerable distinction.

Even in defeat, the also-rans have known success. Though not elected, the votes cast in their favor

showed that many people thought that they deserved to be in public office. The fact that there was a contest demonstrated that the minority could express its opinion. Many a good campaign brought the issues more clearly into focus. In several instances changes advocated by the loser were later incorporated into the working plan of society.

There are those who feel that the greatest victory achieved by the losers is that they refused to give in to apathy. They were willing to expose themselves to the rigors of campaigning. They dared to stand up for what they believed and to denounce what they thought was wrong. They were aware of the price to be paid; but they felt that their cause was worth the effort. They did not sit at home wishing something could be done; they tried to do something they believed in.

Anticipation

There's an old saying, "Anticipation exceeds realization," which indicates that joy need not be confined to any particular occasion. We can have joy looking forward to a happy time, and once we have experienced it memory lives on.

This came sharply into focus for us when during the first week in April we received an invitation to our little granddaughter's birthday party in October. She is looking forward to a "big day" and she wants us to keep it in mind. We are pretty sure she is using some of the cards that were left over from her last birthday. This involves anticipation of a future event, and the memory of a very pleasant birthday party six months in the past.

107

There is also an element of a current pleasure, as she dearly loves writing to her Grandma, and Grandma is equally happy to receive the notes.

This is a beautiful way of stretching the joys of life. However, it is not so good when applied to unpleasant happenings. Dread of a coming event has a power to sour a long period of time. Nurturing slights, hurts, and ill feelings in a dismal bag of memory merely prolongs discomfort and heartache which had been better left in the past.

How we look forward to the future and back at the past determines our philosophy as optimists or pessimists. We may elect to be disillusioned, negative thinkers; or we may take a positive approach to life. Jesus commended the childlike attitude which is built around responsive love, ready confidence, and faith. He never took even a college freshman course in psychology—but how well he knew the human spirit.

What Other Qualifications?

A while back *The Wall Street Journal* carried a meaningful cartoon. It showed the personnel officer of a bank interviewing an applicant, and asking, "What other qualifications do you have besides a genuine love of money?"

A similar cartoon appeared in *Key,* the diocesan newspaper for Kansas City and St. Joseph. It showed two angels sitting on a cloud watching another angel, who was sitting all alone on another cloud busily counting the contents of a large moneybag. One watcher was saying, "Looks like Harry took it with him."

One man said, "If I can't take it with me I don't

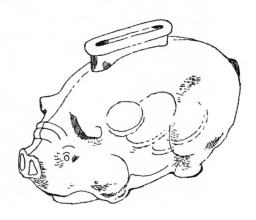

want to go." It was said as a joke but may have expressed his real devotion.

The religions of the world eschew the amassing of a great fortune as a way of life. Giving a tithe, and often a second tithe, is required by many faith groups. Making a sacrifice, rather than a fortune, is the acceptable way. Some clergy take a vow of poverty along with vows of chastity and obedience.

When men and women with great wealth have a matching greatness of spirit, though, great things are done for the good of mankind. This is on a higher level than gifts made with a view toward building a better public image or a profitable tax adjustment. What's the gift without the giver?

This opens the door to all of us. The senior citizen on a small pension, the young person starting a new family, and the wealthiest person alive all have the same potential. All may have the same concern for people and all may express that concern. If there is a divine ledger, it probably records the spirit of giving rather than the amounts given.

Too Much of a Good Thing

It has been said that the younger generation is living proof that a person can thrive on a diet of hot dogs, hamburgers, pizzas, potato chips, candy bars, and ice cream. It is better to eat freaky junk food than to freak out as junkies.

Some of us remember how sweet it was to dip into Grandma's cookie jar. We enjoyed licking the dasher when the home-made ice cream was starting to firm up. How good it was when we could have the leftover frosting when Mama made another cake! And what ambrosia when we spread a thick layer of butter on a slice of bread still hot from the baking. Now, with the bulge of a protracted middle-aged spread, flabby mus-

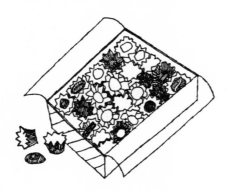

cles, and cholesterol-plugged blood vessels, we wonder if we didn't have too much of a good thing.

It reminds us of the "Boston Molasses Flood" back in 1919, when a wooden tank holding two and a half million gallons of the sticky sweet gave way. It could have been used to make many palate-pleasing things, ranging from pancake topping to a sturdy New England rum. Let loose all at once, it wrought havoc: freight cars were toppled, tracks were uprooted, property damaged. Fifteen people died in that eight-foot wave of molasses. (*Yankee Magazine,* January 1965.)

Rich foods, leisure-time pleasures, travel, reading, listening to good music are all great. In too big a dose they are like another wave of molasses, and they are deadly. We can find a happy balance in work, creativity, and helpfulness.

The Burden of Aging

In an agrarian society old people continue to make their contribution to the welfare of the family. It used to be good to have Grandpa help with the crops and Grandma help with the canning. But times have changed, and the pressure of our society has changed "that nice old person" from an asset to a liability. Recent reports show that a little over 5 percent of the average worker's pay goes into Social Security, and that this will double in about fifty years.

Senior citizens are pleased to hear of any rise in their Social Security benefits. We should keep in mind the mounting resentment among younger people who are unhappy about the rising tax bite needed to support the

system. Signs of the rebellion are apparent in the repeated defeats of almost all proposed tax increases or special bond issues. We hear grumblings against the many things done for the aged. There are those who are troubled about the growth of our "gray power" as we become an increasingly large part of the population. It is possible that ageism will find a place beside racism and sexism.

Mature wisdom should be telling us to be more concerned with how we can contribute to our society and less concerned with making demands upon it. Tax breaks, senior citizen's discounts, free bus rides, free checking accounts, free trash collection, and all those other "freebies" have to be paid for by someone. Let us think of ways in which we can help as well as be helped.

Socially Acceptable Sins

It is so easy to look through the pages of history and be critical of our predecessors. Often they conformed to the existing moral code, but their acts would be frowned upon today. The Puritans crossed the Atlantic to enjoy religious freedom but denied that freedom to those who held different views. Quakers were harassed. Roger Williams was banished from the colony during a bitterly cold New England winter. All of this was rationalized by the conviction that no leaven of unorthodoxy could be tolerated.

The ethics of the 1800's permitted Captain John Harwins to own a slave ship named *Jesus*. Captain John Newton, another slaver, composed the hymn "How Sweet the Name of Jesus Sounds" while his ship lay at

anchor off the coast of Africa, awaiting a cargo of slaves.

We raise our eyebrows at their rationalizations, for we have a different code of ethics. But we are equally smitten by the "everybody does it" syndrome and we rationalize our shortcomings with comparable skill.

A widow fears to leave her house at night because the streets are unsafe. She sees someone siphoning gas from a neighbor's car, but does not call the police—she doesn't want to get involved and expose herself to possible reprisals.

We thank God for our prosperity, assuming that we deserve it by dint of resourcefulness and hard work. It must therefore follow that the poor deserve to be poor.

An ancient prayer asked for help with those "sins which easily beset us." These have been called the socially acceptable sins, the ones that don't jolt society. But in the long run sins are sins. Perhaps the most dangerous sins are those of which we are least aware.

I Think I Can . . .

One of the joys of being a grandparent is having a little tot climb up onto your lap and ask you to read a story. There is an old favorite which my grandchildren like, just the way their parents did. A little locomotive was faced with a long, difficult uphill climb. He was able to make it because he kept puffing, "I *think* I can . . . I *think* I can . . . I *think* I can."

That is the spirit which is crowned with success. It is an attitude which we can take to heart. Even more than what a person eats, what he thinks is what he becomes. Apparently that was what Paul had in mind when he wrote to the church at Philippi. He listed a number of virtues and then urged his readers to "think about these things." That admonition comes to us to-

day in varying accents and settings: "Think about these things!"

I learned a pertinent lesson from the patients in one of our mental hospitals. One ward's population consisted of a number of deeply disturbed women whose behavior was a serious problem. The ward government suggested having a very special party at which relatives of the patients would be guests. It was a success. As hostesses, the patients received their guests with graciousness. The patients were properly groomed and well-behaved. It had been thought that they would be "ladies," and they were.

It is amazing what you can do when someone has faith in you. We can have faith in ourselves and become the persons that God wants us to be.

Let George Do It

George is a popular figure. He is that mythical person who is supposed to do all the things that ought to be done that no one wants to do. The trouble is that no one has identified George.

Leaving it to George means that we ask why the government isn't doing something about a problem. It is referring a sticky situation to a committee. It is suggesting that industry, or some wealthy person, rise to the situation and meet a given need. Doing this, we think that we are relieved of responsibility and that the burden of guilt is cast upon others.

As ponderously slow as governmental agencies may be I still believe they are trying. Industry is giving evidence of corporate conscience. A good example was found in a recent annual report of a large corporation, which announced that it had spent $273.8 million on

environmental protection. Are we equally responsible?

It has been demonstrated that slower driving saves fuel and lives. No representative of a government agency, no policeman, has his foot on the gas pedal in our cars. Religious bodies have an impact on the moral conscience of the community; but no clergyman can be "good" on behalf of his flock. The rabbi from Nazareth suggested that no contribution from the wealthy businessman is equal to the "widow's mite."

Beneficial changes in society and the structure of moral integrity are the outgrowth of a hunger for righteousness in people like you and me. Some things cannot be delegated to others—such as the responsibility that is clearly ours. No George is likely to appear to do what I ought to do.

Did You Ever Wonder Why . . .?

There are many things that we simply take for granted without ever asking why they are done the way they are.

As a part of the national observance of the Bicentennial, it was suggested to American Baptist churches that they might use a model of corporate worship which was used by Baptists in colonial America. The suggestion included the note: "Because it was considered necessary for an ordained elder to be present for the Lord's Supper, and because most churches shared a minister with three or four other congregations, each had a minister present about once a month. Baptists, therefore, celebrated Communion on a monthly basis." Thus a habit, or tradition, was established on a practical, rather than a theological, basis.

Put your mind to work—keep asking questions—it is a good experience trying to find the answers. I offer

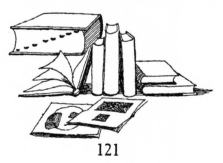

121

a few questions for you to look up or dredge out of your memory:

Why does a man tip his hat to a lady, or remove it in an elevator?

Why does a Jew wear a hat at prayers?

Why do we use the right hand in a handshake?

Why do men's coats have buttons on the cuffs?

Why do we spank a child on his birthday?

Why is there a red-and-white striped pole at the barber shop?

Why is the shamrock associated with the Irish?

You can ask yourself hundreds of questions and keep a lively interest until you are a hundred and ten. (By the way, the answers to the questions above will *not* be found on any page in this book.) Have fun.

Howdy, Ma'am

The sports section of our paper showed a picture of Steve Grady of the Los Angeles Dodgers as he jogged into first base. He greeted the umpire, Christine Wren, with a polite "Howdy, ma'am." The same edition of the paper carried a story saying that Pat Head, coach of the University of Tennessee's women's basketball team, now has four new four-year athletic scholarships for members of her team.

A feature story recently announced that Jane Cheney Spock now is given credit as coauthor with her

ex-husband, Dr. Benjamin Spock, for the writing of the popular book on the care of children. She explained that when the book was first published it wasn't considered "proper" for a wife to claim her right to recognition.

When I was a youngster I was a member of the Junior Navy. It was something like the Boy Scouts except that we developed our skills and learned our morals on Narragansett Bay. Our "ship" was under the care of one of the town's prominent women, an activist in the early part of the century. Naturally, she persuaded us to march in the protest parade advocating women's suffrage.

Oldsters sometimes are disturbed when things are not the way they used to be. Not all change is for the better, nor are all the old ways to be despised. But changes that liberate and fulfill should be affirmed. I say, "Howdy, ma'am, you've come a long way."

Leisure Time

Soon after my grandmother moved to New England from central Canada, the fishmonger's wagon stopped in front of her home. His horn drew her to her upstairs piazza. She asked what was especially good and he recommended some of his freshly caught swordfish. Being from freshwater fish country, she ordered two "if they are of good size." He stared for a moment and then blurted out, "Are you sure that will be enough?"

A friend who had moved here from Europe enjoyed telling of her introduction to our vegetables. She saw sweet corn, which appealed to her, so she bought two ears. She laughingly tells of cooking it for hours in a vain attempt to get the center tender.

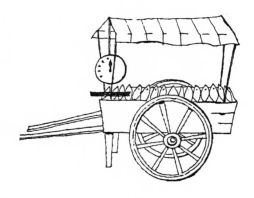

125

Retirement is like moving into a new world. We are faced with the problem of leisure time. While working at our profession, a vacation, a free weekend, or a few hours in the evening offered a leisure that was refreshing. Full-time leisure is a different "kettle of fish," comparable to Grandma's idea of lake trout when she was asking for half a ton of swordfish.

Leisure may be akin to my friend's overcooked sweet corn. If leisure isn't handled correctly it is never softened. The lesson we learn from retirement is to use our time in proper amounts and use it well. We learn there is a difference between scrambling for entertainment and finding the peace which passes understanding. We learn to pass up the cheap thrill and enjoy truly meaningful relationships and activities. Our prayer simmers down to a simple petition: "Lord, help us to know what to look for, and to use what we find. Amen."

Take Time to Talk

The long cattle drives from Texas would have been impossible without the chuckwagons which were a part of each outfit. As a center of activity, the chuckwagon gave the drovers a whole lot more than beans, bacon, and coffee. Here was a place for conversation. Around "Cookie's" open fire the trailhands gathered to spin yarns, swap lies, and propound their solutions to the problems of the universe. Around the chuckwagon the men fed their bodies with hearty food and their spirits with lively conversation.

We don't have the same life-style that the cowboy had on the trail, but even in this crowded hustle-bustle world of today we can be just as lonely. We have no

herds of cattle, but we are surrounded by droves of people who are so busy getting someplace that they have no time to sit and visit for a while. A generation ago there was more time for friends. Today's supermarket has no potbellied stove or checkers game. They have even taken the whittlin' bench from in front of the courthouse.

Good conversation is of even greater value than the enjoyment it gives us. Conversation is a means for the meeting of minds. It provides the kind of give-and-take that builds mutual respect. Strengthened by honesty and a shared trust, it becomes the best tool to remove the piques and barriers which may have grown up between friends or family members. Jesus told his disciples that reconciliation with an estranged friend (or family member) was a prerequisite to an acceptable religious offering. Take time to talk.

Snow

Today the world looks like a Christmas card. Ever so silently, snow has fallen, touching up roofs and decorating the trees and shrubs. Everything wears immaculate, diamond-studded white vestments in preparation for the celebration of the sacrament of winter.

Snow, so soft and beautiful, possesses an amazing strength. A little snow can make cars crawl and cause many persons to be late to work; a number of cars will be driven home with accordion-pleated fenders. A lot of snow can paralyze a region.

Television and radio announcers read long lists of

129

schools that will be closed for the day—it is too risky to take the school buses out on the streets and highways. Joy reigns supreme in the hearts of children. Kids who have been wearily plodding through the three R's will romp in the new snow. They see themselves as hardy pioneers as they make tracks through uncharted and unbroken wilderness.

Some of the children become sculptors. A feminist spirit is seen—there are as many snow-women as snowmen.

Other children become military strategists, building snow forts and stockpiling snowballs. This is an acceptable kind of warfare, as the only casualty is snow down the neck, or soggy mittens which Grandma can replace.

Snow is great fun for the children, but it is not quite so welcome to us oldsters who worry about a bad fall. And it poses a problem for those who have walks to clear. But snow also brings out the goodness in people. Several times we have found our walk and driveway cleared by kindly young neighbors.

Snow quietly covers the earth and blankets its ugliness and scars with a pristine purity. In a similar way kindness, understanding, and love can radiate from wrinkled old faces, and arthritic hands can be busy doing acts of kindness.

Is This the Time?

When the Continental Congress was considering the question of making a declaration of independence, the delegates had marked differences of opinion. Some called for immediate action; others hesitated, thinking that it would be folly to dissociate the colonies from the protection afforded them by the army and navy of Great Britain. And, as usual, there were the timid, who agreed in principle but wondered if the time was right to make so drastic a move.

I have attended many meetings at which the age-old question has been raised: "Is this the right time?" In some cases timing is of strategic importance. But often

the question "Is this the time?" is simply a delaying tactic expressing a timid, negative attitude which is a barnacle on the keel of progress.

Never think that this great inhibitor is at work only in government, in church meetings, or in clubs and societies. This form of temporization often keeps us from knowing the fullness of life as individuals.

It is a tragedy to retire from life as well as from a job. Now is the time to do all those beautiful things we always thought we were too busy to do. Now is the time to tell someone that you love her or him and to reinforce that declaration by doing a kindly deed. Now is the time to write a newsy letter to a lonely or depressed friend. Better still, now is the time to make that visit you have been thinking about. Now is the time to say "Thank you." Now is the time to volunteer to work at a hospital, or in a Meals On Wheels program, or wherever your talents fill a need. Now is the time to live at your highest potential.

Holding a Grudge?

I was rocked back on my heels when a middle-aged woman asked me to pray away her brother's salvation. She reasoned that he had it coming, because long ago he had treated her meanly. For thirty years she had been holding a grudge—hugging it close to her bosom, cherishing it, letting it gnaw away at her. It is possible that the brother never knew of the loathing and hate which she had for him. The hurt had all been accomplished on the woman herself.

A doctor friend asked me to see a patient of his, as he felt that her problem was religious. She was emo-

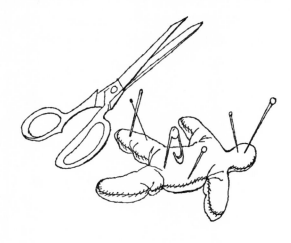

tionally immobilized by a fear of the punishment which God would inflict upon her. He suggested that I talk to her about the grace offered by a God of love, mercy, and forgiveness. I thought that I did a good job in giving her the Scriptural tools from which she might fashion the key to unlock that love for herself. In the next session she smugly produced a two-page list of Scripture passages telling of the wrath of God and the punishment he metes out. She was projecting onto God all the grudges she held against many people, including herself.

Jesus clarified the matter when he explained that if we are about to approach God and remember that things are not right between us and a friend or member of the family, that it behooves us to talk it out and make things right with that person, thus opening the way to God. (See Matt. 5:23–24.) Holding a grudge clutters and obstructs the path to God's presence. And besides, it makes us miserable and hard to live with.

Never the Twain Shall Meet

We hear that there is an unbridgeable gap which separates cultures and generations within cultures. Kipling's line "East is East and West is West and never the twain shall meet" has been applied to the generation gap. We may even have been sold on the idea that we all would be happier if senior citizens could live in retirement centers which are really "gray ghettos"— the theory being that those living in retirement centers will not be annoyed by the younger generation, and the old folks would be kept out of the hair of the young.

There is an opposite philosophy which has proved itself by bearing some mighty fine fruit. Senior citizens

may earn a little money by working as "foster grandparents." These men and women give of themselves and their time in close relationship with autistic children, or children who have been slow in the development of normal skills. A growing love between child and adult frequently becomes the catalyst in an alchemy by which both are enriched.

Our church provides a needed day care center for the children of working mothers. Great things are happening, not the least of which is what it has done for two older ladies. The wife of a retired clergyman enjoys the contact with the children as she prepares their daily lunches. Working by her side is a resettled Vietnamese grandmother who finds the fellowship enriching and a pleasant way to build her vocabulary in the language of her new country.

The generations really need each other. By using a little imagination and working at it in the spirit of love, we find that there are many ways in which the twain may meet.

Sanctuary

To call the church a "sanctuary" is in some ways the worst thing that could happen. This is especially true if we think of a sanctuary as a place where wild animals are herded together. With the best of intentions, the poor creatures are deprived of their freedom, and they become more and more dependent on their keepers. They can no longer fend for themselves.

In a better sense of the word, the church can be and is a sanctuary to which people may flee to escape "the world, the flesh and the devil." In spiritual and physical danger they may find safety, as did Joab, by grasping "the horns of the altar" (I Kings 2:28 ff.).

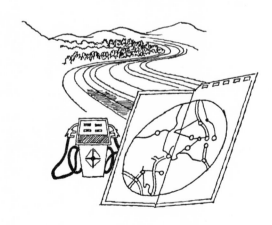

Emma Lazarus seems to express the message of the church in the inscription on the Statue of Liberty, in which she says: "Give me your tired, your poor, your huddled masses yearning to breathe free . . ."

The church is indeed a refuge for those whose strength falters, whose hopes dim, and whose courage fails. But this is a temporary stop, not the end of the journey. To make the sanctuary our home is to retreat from living. Our need is not only to be loved, but to love; not only to be served, but to serve; not only to get, but to give.

The church might be compared to a gas station. It affords a stop for a moment's rest after a hard drive on the throughway. Here we can find a map to be sure we are on the right road, and here we can be refueled to keep on toward our destination.

I'm Shocked

A cartoon in *The Wall Street Journal* shows two women having tea. One is saying, "Every now and again I'm shocked at the things that don't shock me anymore."

Missouri Congressman Jerry Litton mailed a rather long questionnaire to his constituents. The answers were tabulated according to several age brackets of the respondents. It appeared that younger people were rigid moral idealists who recognized no gray shades between right and wrong. Older people gave answers that reflected more tolerance and forgiveness, as if they had been influenced by Joseph Fletcher's "situation ethics." Maybe we older folks are more aware of our own weaknesses and failures, and less ready to criticize the shortcomings of others.

On the other hand, we may simply be reflecting a general erosion in the moral structure of our society. The current tendency is to bring secret sins out into the open. Dirty linen is hung out in the front yard and not hidden in a back closet. A way of living which used to be frowned upon is accepted as "the way of life for today." Words which were never uttered in the presence of ladies are now used by the ladies themselves. Pleasure has taken the place of purity, and profit has usurped the place of pride.

It need not be so. There is a difference between being judgmental and having good judgment. We need not drift with the tide. There is value in being shocked enough to recognize that it is time to put out the anchor and thus avoid the rocks of moral destruction.

The Lord Is My Strength

The doctor had explained that the best treatment for my heart condition was to be sure to get plenty of rest and avoid the strain of severely cold weather and strong winds. I think that my wife, Ruth, took this even more seriously than I did.

One morning when the temperature had dropped to fifteen degrees, she muffled up to get the morning paper and leave the outgoing mail in the roadside mailbox. When she came back into the house, there was snow on the back of her coat. It took a while for her to admit that she had actually fallen.

141

What if her fall had resulted in a broken hip rather than a snow-covered hip? She did her best to get me to promise that should she fall again, I would not come out to get her. Instead, I was to phone one of the neighbors for help.

What utter frustration that would create! How would I ever be able to leave her, hurt and in the cold, while I sought help from others? I am convinced that if such a situation were to occur I would be given strength to do what was needed.

Centuries ago an ancient hymn writer expressed my belief. In Psalm 118 we read: "I was pushed hard, so that I was falling, but the Lord helped me. The Lord is my strength and my song." Faith is mighty powerful adrenalin.

One Image of Old Age

"An old man, sitting under a shade tree on a sunny day, gives good advice. But in the middle of a terrible storm, count on him for nothing." This is what one high school student wrote in *Reflections,* a school paper published in our town.

Is this a true reflection of what oldsters are like? Or are the youngsters getting a distorted image because ours is a youth-centered era? Apparently the heroes of today are the bra-less sweater girl and the muscular football player. Practically illiterate athletes command far better salaries than teachers, preachers, or artists.

Good counselors have been trained to assist people by listening and helping them to work out their own

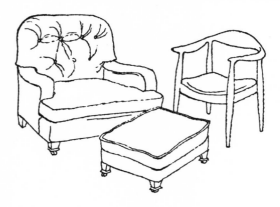

problems. The counselor (the old man under the shade tree) is not a giver of advice. He becomes the one in whom people may confide. This may be our role as senior citizens, letting people think out loud. We can let them try new concepts on us for size before committing themselves to specific action. Age should have helped us to be more shockproof and understanding than we used to be.

That writer in *Reflections* shouldn't expect grandparents to be stacking sandbags along the riverbank during a flood or tornado. But in other storms (emotional, financial, and family) we may have a contribution to make. In a time of strife it is good to know that someone will stand at our side. Perhaps it is our role to stand by and show understanding, love, and concern. This may be the help most needed.

Sursum Corda

A deeply depressed young man was being interviewed by a treatment team at the hospital to which he had recently been admitted. The staff members were looking for the best way to help this man, who felt that the bottom had dropped out of his world and left him hopeless.

A cultured Jewish doctor from Vienna presided at the meeting. When he learned that the patient had been a devout Roman Catholic, the doctor quoted a phrase from the Latin mass: *"Sursum corda"*—"Lift up your heart." This brought the first visible response from the severely withdrawn young man.

A responsive chord had been struck. It was as if he

were regaining some of the assurance and faith voiced in the Twenty-seventh Psalm. The psalmist felt that, even if friends and family should let him down, the Lord would pick him up. This basic faith in the goodness of God who would lift his heart was the psalmist's theme.

You usually don't expect a hospital staff meeting to provide a religious experience, but I believe that is what happened. Who can tell when the right word will be spoken to give us the heart to function at our very best and in the spirit of confidence?

The Anxious Seat

Hospital administrators know the intense feeling we have when a loved one is in the operating room or the intensive care unit. To help, they have provided attractive waiting rooms which are as close to the patients as possible. The "ladies in cherry red" (the volunteers) are understanding and supportive. They have an urn of freshly brewed coffee and the magazines are even of recent issue.

To be a part of the waiting group is exhausting; anxiety, apprehension, and tension drain you. Every

time the door opens, you study any staff member making an appearance. Finally, the surgeon comes to give a report on his findings. His every gesture is weighed and interpreted as a "good" or a "bad" sign. If he is tired and wipes his brow with a touch of a frown, hearts and hopes drop. How you hang on to his words as he tells of the operation and the prognosis! Many times the report is good, and then hope and joy are manifest. But there are times when the news he must bring is not good.

The pastor or the friend who cares enough to be with you is loved and long remembered. From time to time we may be allowed to show our loving concern by being at the side of our friends. A shared burden is easier to bear.

Remember that when Jesus was facing betrayal and arrest he needed the strength which he found in private prayers in Gethsemane. As personal as that experience was, he needed also three disciples to stand by. He was hurt when they dozed during his hour of crisis.

"Couldn't you watch for even an hour?" was a valid question then, and it is today.

Lights at the Neighbor's

It's a good feeling to see lights at a neighbor's window. A light seems to say that all is well. People are enjoying the evening with conversation, reading a good book, watching television, or entertaining guests. When the lights are on at an unusual time you wonder whether there is sickness. If someone is ill, it's good to think that one member of the family probably is lending a helping hand. A lighted window lets us share vicariously in the human encounter when we care for "the people next door."

Ours is an age of restless mobility, in which a fixed place of residence has become a rarity. I tend to appreciate the staying qualities of my aunt who lived all of

her life in the same house. But this is the day when job assignments frequently call for transfers. As I think back I have to admit that the moving van has hauled our furniture off several times. We moved to our retirement home just about five years ago and we have already seen several of our neighbors move away. (No, they didn't take a look at us and say "There goes the neighborhood!")

After a neighboring family has moved out, the vacant house appears to be in a period of mourning. No reflected lights on the windowshades erase the sad darkness. The empty house appears to share our hope that the new occupants will be friendly people. We are challenged to do something to ensure that they will. We remember that it has been said that we usually find the kind of people that we are looking for. As a part of the established community we now have a responsibility to offer the new people a friendly welcome and let them know that we want them in our community as neighbors and friends.

Preparing for Old Age

Retirement brings an emotional shock for those who haven't prepared for it. Knowing this, one church arranged for a series of breakfast meetings for those anticipating retirement. They discussed their plans, their hopes, and their fears about their later years. It was their conclusion that retirement is richer for those who prepare for it.

You don't suddenly drop into a new life-style without learning some of the rules of the game. Here are a few rules or guidelines for your consideration:

Continue to develop your spiritual life. Rather than using your religion as a "preparation for your finals," see how much meaning it can give to living day by day.

Keep up your activities, especially those hobbies

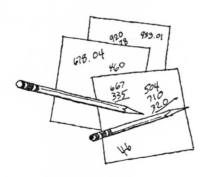

151

which bring you into relationship with old and new friends. Idleness is boring.

Maintain your friendships even if it is done through letter-writing or phone calls. Isolation breeds stagnation.

Carefully budget your financial resources. Check with authorities about your Social Security benefits and other dependable income *before retirement.* Be sure to maintain a good credit rating. If you move to a new town, establish a working relationship with a bank or a savings and loan association.

Write a will. Even if your resources are limited, get advice from a good lawyer to help you decide how your assets will be used.

Remember your health care. See your doctor and dentist on a regular basis. Consider a supplement to Medicare for possible medical and hospital bills.

Before you sell your home and move to a new community or an apartment, weigh that move carefully. Don't jump too fast.

The car which you bring into retirement should be new or at least mechanically sound.

A prepared retiree is a happier retiree.

You're a Clergyperson Too

Doctor Karl Menninger wrote: "The clergyman is a very special 'someone.' He stands in a special place; he has special authority, not just because he has had education in theology and perhaps in psychology, but because he is 'a man of God.' He is dedicated. He is unselfish. He has no wish to hurt but only to help people—and that is rare! . . . We need him as our umpire, to direct us, to accuse us, to reproach us, to shrive us." (*Whatever Became of Sin?* Hawthorne Books, Inc., 1973.)

We might think of Doctor Karl as one of those totally self-sufficient persons, but he becomes one of us

153

by admitting that he too needs help. After all, why should we be hesitant to admit our needs? But we are all afraid of such an admission. This fear may be lessened if we seek encouragement and counsel from a minister we can trust.

The good doctor's evaluation of true men of God is heartening to the clergy. There is, however, another side of the coin: all people of faith, ordained or lay, are members of the "priesthood of believers." We need not, nor should we, leave the essentials of "religion" to a few professionals. Having found our measure of faith, we all have a responsibility (and the joy) to help other people experience an abundant and meaningful life in God's love.